A Note to Pare....

DK READERS is a compelling program for beginning readers, designed in conjunction with leading literacy experts.

Beautiful illustrations and superb full-color photographs combine with engaging, easy-to-read stories to offer a fresh approach to each subject in the series. Each DK READER is guaranteed to capture a child's interest while developing his or her reading skills, general knowledge, and love of reading.

The four levels of DK READERS are aimed at different reading abilities, enabling you to choose the books that are exactly right for your child:

Level 1 – Beginning to read
Level 2 – Beginning to read alone
Level 3 – Reading alone
Level 4 – Proficient readers

The "normal" age at which a child begins to read can be anywhere from three to eight years old, so these levels are only a general guideline.

No matter which level you select, you can be sure that you are helping your child learn to read, then read to learn!

LONDON, NEW YORK, MELBOURNE,
MUNICH, AND DELHI

Editor Kate Simkins
Designer Sooz Bellerby
Series Editor Alastair Dougall
Production Jenny Jacoby
Picture Researcher Bridget Tily

First American Edition, 2004
04 05 06 07 10 9 8 7 6 5 4 3 2
Published in the United States by DK Publishing, Inc.
375 Hudson Street, New York, New York 10014

Library of Congress Cataloging-in-Publication Data

Donkin, Andrew.
 Transformers Armada : the uprising / by Andrew Donkin.-- 1st
American
ed.
    p. cm. -- (DK readers)
 Summary: Forgetting their rivalry, Autobots and Decepticons join
together in the face of a cosmic enemy--Unicron.
 ISBN 0-7566-0310-2 (PB) -- ISBN 0-7566-0311-0 (HC)
 [1. Science fiction.] I. Title: Uprising. II. Title. III. Series:
Dorling Kindersley readers.
 PZ7.D7175Tt 2004
 [Fic]--dc22

                    2003019545

Color reproduction by Colourscan, Singapore
Printed and bound in China by L Rex Printing Co., Ltd.

The publisher thanks the following for their kind permission
to reproduce their photographs:
c=center; t=top; b=below; l=left; r=right

26 NASA: bl. **29 Orion Press:** cr.

All other photographs © Dorling Kindersley.
For further information see: www.dkimages.com

Discover more at
www.dk.com

Contents

PROFICIENT
4
READERS

The Uprising

Written by Andrew Donkin

Deadly enemies

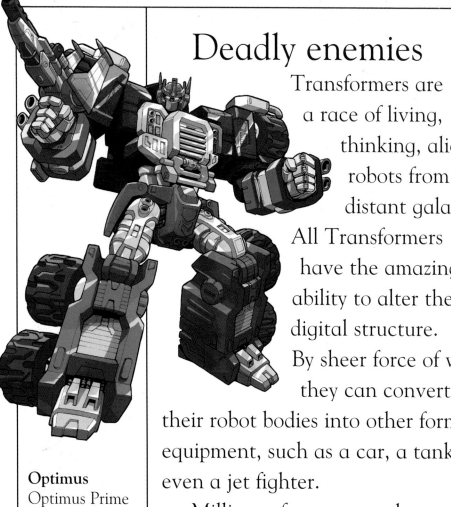

Transformers are a race of living, thinking, alien robots from a distant galaxy. All Transformers have the amazing ability to alter their digital structure. By sheer force of will, they can convert their robot bodies into other forms of equipment, such as a car, a tank, or even a jet fighter.

Millions of years ago, the Transformers split into two factions—the peace-loving Autobots, led by Optimus Prime, and the evil, power-hungry Decepticons, led by Megatron, now known as Galvatron. Soon the two groups were at war, fighting for control of their home planet, Cybertron.

Optimus
Optimus Prime has led his Autobot troops into many battles against the evil Decepticons, but he is now beginning to suspect that the Transformers are merely pawns in a bigger plan.

The Transformers are made up of the giant Autobots and Decepticons and the smaller Mini-Cons.

During the conflict, a signal reached Cybertron revealing the location of a lost race of smaller Transformers called Mini-Cons. When a Transformer combined with a Mini-Con, the larger Transformer's power and strength were greatly increased. The Autobots and Decepticons traced the signal to Earth, and a race began to be the first to find the Mini-Cons…the keys to victory.

Galvatron
In his early battles, he was known as Megatron, but after a massive power boost, he chose the new name Galvatron.

Mini-Cons
Realizing that their power was escalating the Transformers' war, the Mini-Cons left Cybertron. They ended up on Earth, where the kids discovered them.

Soon after their arrival on Earth, the Autobots befriended the kids, Rad, Carlos, Alexis, Fred, and Billy, who had awoken the Mini-Cons from their hibernation. In the months that followed, the Autobots fought the dreaded Decepticons at locations all over Earth. The battles were ferocious and deadly. Some were won, some lost, and still more ended in a stalemate.

Now the battlefield has shifted again. The Decepticons are in possession of the most powerful Mini-Cons and are back on Cybertron.

The kids are on the Autobots' ship heading for Cybertron. They are determined to help the Autobots stop Galvatron from taking control of the planet.

Optimus's spaceship races back to Cybertron in pursuit of Galvatron.

They are intent on finally winning the war. Although the odds are stacked against them, the Autobots and their human friends are giving chase, hoping somehow to save their home world from falling under Galvatron's control.

There are also growing rumors of a dark shadow from the Transformers' distant past. Whispers tell of a returning evil far more dangerous than anything the Transformers have faced before…

Perceptor
When the kids' three Mini-Cons, High Wire, Sureshock, and Grindor combine, they become the supercharged Perceptor— a real lesson in teamwork.

Galvatron will stop at nothing to defeat his Autobot enemies. He enjoys seeing them suffer.

Cybertron
Cybertron is the home planet of the Transformers race. Before the Autobot-Decepticon war, it was a place of great beauty, with fantastic cities shaped from living metal.

Cybertron at war

In his own way, Galvatron was having the time of his life. The leader of the Decepticons surveyed the battlefield and smiled. After four million years of fighting, he could sense victory was near.

Above him in the dark sky, the Decepticon fleet was powering up its weapons to attack the Autobots' silver ships. On the ground below, hundreds of Decepticon warriors were ready to go into action against the ranks of Autobot troops.

"Let's go!" shouted Galvatron, leaping into action, using the Skyboom Shield to protect himself.

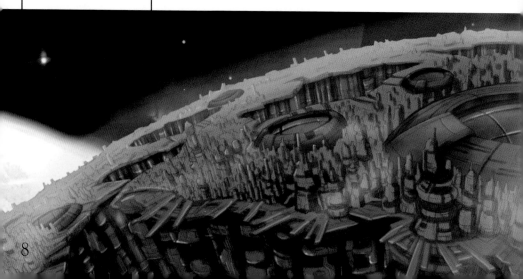

Galvatron took a mighty swing with the Star Saber and sliced clean through one of the Autobot ships. The vessel was consumed in a fiery explosion. Galvatron moved toward his next target as the Autobot ships opened fire.

"All right men, let's dispose of the small fry first. Fire at will!" ordered Galvatron. Light bullets erupted from everywhere, and Galvatron smiled again.

This was going to be very enjoyable battle indeed.

Evil soldiers
The Decepticon warriors are formidable fighters. They are loyal to Galvatron, but only if he brings them victory against the Autobots.

Galvatron gets ready to fire the deadly Requiem Blaster at the Autobots, while protecting himself with the mighty Skyboom Shield.

Thrust and Starscream are hungry for power.

Starscream
This speedy Decepticon likes to think for himself and hates following orders.

Not everyone was quite so happy.

"Galvatron is going to grab all the glory," complained Starscream.

"Let him lead us into battle," snarled Thrust, who was lurking next to Starscream. "With any luck, it will be his last. If you follow my orders, the Universe will be ours, not his!"

It seemed to Starscream that Thrust spent too much time hiding in the shadows scheming, but before Starscream could question him, they came under fire and the moment was lost.

In jet mode, Starscream can unleash terrifying attacks from above.

Millions of light-years away, Optimus's ship was speeding through space toward Cybertron.

The atmosphere on the bridge was tense. Everyone was anxious to reach the Transformers' home world before it was too late.

"Long-range scanners show that the worst fighting is in the northern polar region. We can land there and go straight into battle against the enemy," suggested Blurr.

"No, it's too obvious," said Optimus. "That's exactly what Galvatron will be expecting us to do. We'll need a better plan…"

Blurr
When it comes to action, Blurr doesn't take any prisoners. The Autobot's cool head sometimes puts him at odds with Hot Shot.

Optimus looks out anxiously from the bridge of his ship. It is a race against time to reach Cybertron and try to stop Galvatron's evil plans.

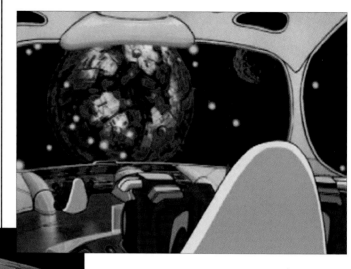

As their ship approaches Cybertron, the Autobots are dismayed to see the terrible war raging on its surface.

Collapsing star
A black hole is formed when a star reaches the end of its life and collapses. Not even light can escape from a black hole.

A few hours later, the Autobots' ship came streaking out of warp space. At last, Optimus Prime and his Autobot team were nearing home.

The kids rushed to the ship's window to get their first view of the mysterious planet.

"So that's Cybertron!" said Rad.

"It looks so peaceful from up here," said Alexis.

"It might look peaceful, but each one of those lights flickering on the surface is a battlefield," Optimus Prime reminded them.

Then the crew spotted something else—behind Cybertron's bleak, cratered moon was an object none of the Autobots had expected to see.

The Mini-Cons alert the Autobots to the danger of Unicron.

"That's a black hole! And it's dangerously close to the planet!" said Optimus Prime.

The Mini-Cons on the bridge began to panic and wave their arms.

"They say it's the work of something evil called Unicron!" reported Rad.

"We'll have to find out more from the Mini-Cons later," said Optimus Prime. "Right now, we have to get down to the planet!"

Black hole
Many scientists believe that there may be a black hole right at the center of our own galaxy, the Milky Way. Black holes are hard to detect because they cannot be seen directly.

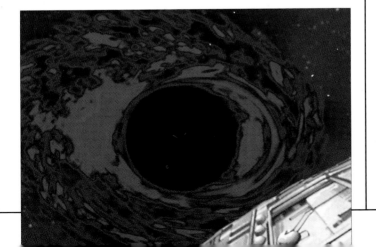

A gaping black hole threatens to swallow up Cybertron.

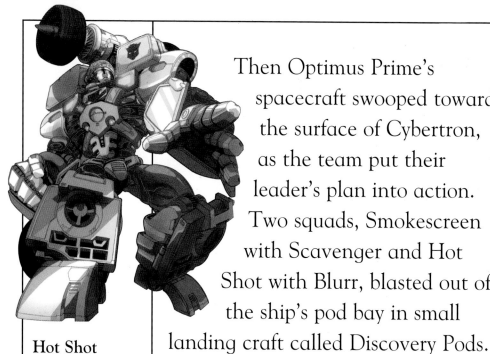

Then Optimus Prime's spacecraft swooped toward the surface of Cybertron, as the team put their leader's plan into action. Two squads, Smokescreen with Scavenger and Hot Shot with Blurr, blasted out of the ship's pod bay in small landing craft called Discovery Pods.

A scene of utter devastation greeted them on the surface.

"Man, this place is a disaster area!" said Smokescreen, looking around in horror.

Hot Shot
Hot Shot is second-in-command to Optimus and has taken charge of Autobot forces in several past battles.

Looking for signs of life, the Autobot search party lands on Cybertron.

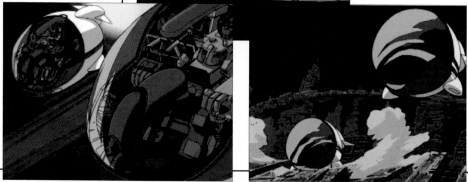

The war had reduced the Transformers' once-flourishing planet to a wasteland.

"Can anyone hear me?" shouted Hot Shot.

The teams split up to search for survivors. Hot Shot and Blurr transformed into vehicle mode and raced along a highway. Meanwhile, Optimus arrived on the planet and, in Jet Prime mode, flew over the once-beautiful city.

Suddenly Optimus saw movement in the dark sky above. Speeding toward them was the entire Decepticon fleet, led by their mighty leader, Galvatron.

"Nice of you to join us!" snarled Galvatron, getting ready to attack. "At least now we'll be able to bury you on your home planet!"

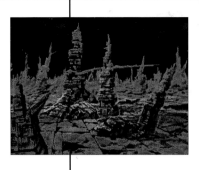

All the terrible wars on Cybertron have left the glittering planet in ruins.

Fast wheels
When he transforms, Hot Shot becomes a sleek yellow sports car, which makes him one of the fastest ground-based Transformers.

The Decepticons opened fire, pinning down Optimus and his men.

"Optimus super mode, transform!"

Super Optimus
When Optimus combines with his trailer, he becomes an even more powerful version of himself called Super Optimus Prime.

said Optimus, powerlinking with the Mini-Con Overload.

Optimus's twin laser cannons opened fire and blasted two attacking Decepticon ships right out of the sky.

The entire planet seemed to shake as several dozen Autobot ships suddenly rose out of their hiding places under the rubble.

"Awesome! There are survivors—and lots of them!" said Hot Shot.

As the Autobot ships emerge from the wreckage, Optimus takes advantage of the surprise and opens fire on the Decepticons with his laser cannons.

The sky glows red from thousands of Transformer light bullets as the ships fire at each other.

Overload
Optimus Prime's first Mini-Con partner was Sparkplug, but Prime later teamed up with the even more powerful Overload.

The two massive space fleets opened fire on each other, and a blaze of crimson light bullets flashed through Cybertron's sky.

Above the battle something strange was happening. Several hundred Mini-Cons were floating through space toward the black hole. The Mini-Cons wanted to help the Autobots. They knew that the black hole was about to cause even more problems than Galvatron.

Back on the planet below, Galvatron activated the Star Saber and leaped toward Optimus Prime with the deadly weapon raised.

The Mini-Cons try to save Cybertron from the black hole.

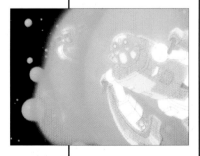

Optimus tries to persuade Galvatron that they should join forces to defeat Unicron.

Sideways
There's more to this warrior than meets the eye. Who is he really working for?

Optimus caught hold of Galvatron's arm and blocked his attack.

"Enough!" said Optimus. "This war isn't just about you and me. According to the Mini-Cons, an ancient evil is returning, a force called Unicron, and neither of us can stop it alone."

"Unicron doesn't exist. He's just a legend, a horror story told to frighten half-witted Autobots like you!" Galvatron sneered.

"I don't know much about Unicron, but I have a hunch that somehow that troublemaker Sideways is involved. I think Unicron created that black hole up there" said Optimus.

Both enemies looked into the darkening sky to see green static crackling like lightning across the face of the black hole.

The ground started to shake, and suddenly a huge chunk of the planet's crust broke loose. The black hole was attacking Cybertron!

Cyberton's moon
Cybertron is orbited by one bleak, cratered moon that moves slowly through the dark Cybertron sky. Is the moon natural or does it hide a sinister secret from the past?

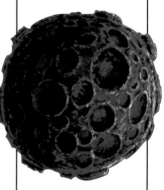

The Mini-Cons move nearer to the black hole.

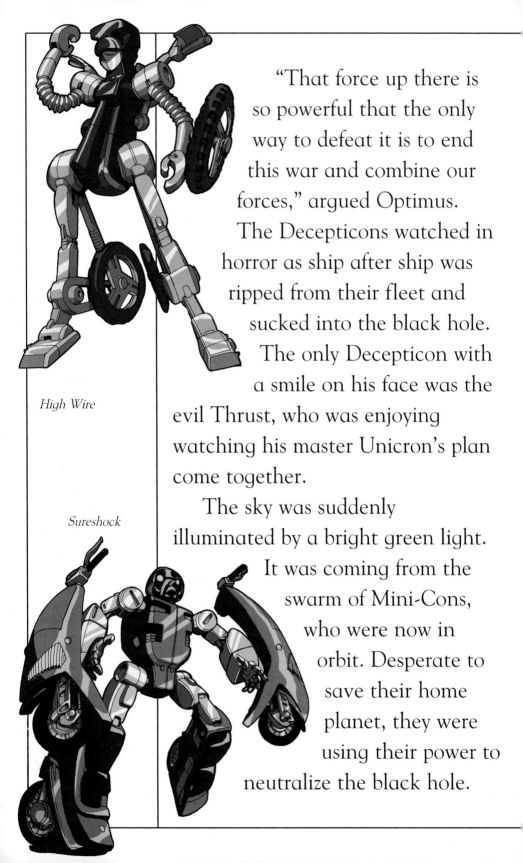

High Wire

Sureshock

"That force up there is so powerful that the only way to defeat it is to end this war and combine our forces," argued Optimus.

The Decepticons watched in horror as ship after ship was ripped from their fleet and sucked into the black hole. The only Decepticon with a smile on his face was the evil Thrust, who was enjoying watching his master Unicron's plan come together.

The sky was suddenly illuminated by a bright green light. It was coming from the swarm of Mini-Cons, who were now in orbit. Desperate to save their home planet, they were using their power to neutralize the black hole.

As their light poured into the black hole, shrinking it to nearly nothing, everyone on the planet heard the Mini-Cons' voices in their head, saying:

"Stop the fighting. Stop the fighting."

Despite what he had seen, Galvatron still refused to believe that Optimus Prime was telling him the truth, and he and his men suddenly warped out of the battlefield. For the moment at least, the war was over.

Grindor

Mini partners
Discovered by the kids in a mountain cave on Earth, High Wire, Sureshock, and Grindor soon became firm friends with their human partners Rad, Carlos, and Alexis.

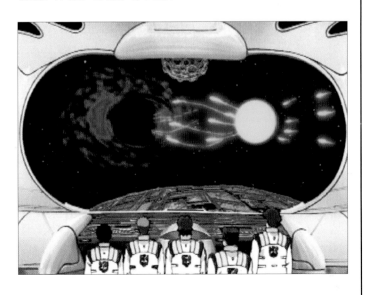

The kids watch as the Mini-Cons use their power to stop the black hole from swallowing the planet Cybertron.

Wheeljack
Long ago back on Cybertron, Wheeljack used to be good friends with Hot Shot. After Galvatron saved his life, however, he joined the Decepticons, fighting against Hot Shot and his Autobot comrades.

Hot Shot creeps into the Decepticon base on a vital mission.

The situation on Cybertron looked grim for Optimus Prime and his Autobots. The Decepticon forces were in control of the surface of the planet, while the black hole was following Cybertron's only moon through the skies above.

Deciding that time was running out for all the Transformers, Hot Shot left the Autobot ship on a deadly solo mission—to convince Galvatron that the Transformers should unite against their common enemy, Unicron.

Sneaking through the Decepticon front line, Hot Shot made a daring raid upon Galvatron's base on Cybertron.

It was a raid that was to change the Transformers' war forever.

Hot Shot encountered Wheeljack first, and as the two of them fought, they smashed through the wall of the Decepticon command room.

"What is the meaning of this outrage?" demanded Galvatron, glaring at Hot Shot.

"Sir, this Autobot has fought his way into our base. He says that he must speak to you!" reported Wheeljack urgently.

Galvatron activated the Star Saber and leaped toward Hot Shot, raising the sword to slice him in two.

Galvatron can't believe an Autobot has the nerve to break into his base.

Hot Shot risks his life to try and save his planet from Unicron's evil plan.

*Wheeljack blocks
Galvatron's blow,
saving Hot Shot.*

Thrust
Thrust is
a veteran
Decepticon
warrior and is
an expert on
military
strategy.

Suddenly Wheeljack blocked the deadly blow, saving Hot Shot's life.

"Sir, I would never betray you, but I beg you to listen to what he has to say!" pleaded Wheeljack. Like many of the other Decepticons, he was worried about the Unicron rumors.

Galvatron reluctantly lowered the Star Saber.

"What!" screamed Thrust. "You must destroy him! Don't listen to his lies, Galvatron!"

But Galvatron had decided that he *would* listen. Hot Shot told him everything that the Autobots had learned about their common foe, Unicron. As he spoke, Thrust looked more and more uneasy.

He tried to interrupt Hot Shot several times with comments about the weapons made from Mini-Cons.

"You look very nervous, Thrust. What's going on? What have you been plotting? And why is it that you know so much about these Mini-Con weapons?" demanded Galvatron suspiciously.

Thrust suddenly grabbed the Skyboom Shield and the Requiem Blaster. He knew the game was up.

Inferno
Inferno was chosen personally by Thrust to be his Mini-Con.

Thrust seems to know more about Unicron than he is letting on.

The Requiem Blaster is one of the weapons the evil Thrust steals from Galvatron.

Galvatron is furious at Thrust's betrayal.

Hurricanes
A hurricane is a revolving storm with inwardly spiraling winds that move quickly around a calm central area, called "the eye." A hurricane usually brings lightning and torrential rain.

"Galvatron, you were never worthy of controlling the Transformers! I've got news for all of you! You're nothing compared to my true master, Unicron!" shouted Thrust with venom.

"What! You miserable traitor!" exclaimed Galvatron, shocked to his hard drive.

"I need all three Mini-Con weapons for my master, but I guess two out of three will have to do for now!" called Thrust.

Then Thrust activated the blades on his back, creating a powerful wind tunnel and slamming Hot Shot and the Decepticons to the far side of the room. While they were pinned down, Thrust made his escape, taking the Skyboom Shield and the Requiem Blaster with him.

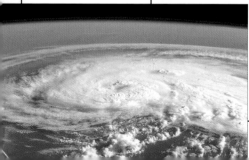

Galvatron was furious.

"Thrust has fled into the underground tunnels! Find him! Find him, if it's the last thing you do!" screamed Galvatron.

Hot Shot and Wheeljack transformed into vehicle mode and began searching the maze of underground passages for the traitor. Starscream, bitter and angry at Thrust's betrayal, was also on his trail.

At least now they had exposed the real enemy— Thrust and his evil master Unicron.

Thrust creates a forceful draft so he can trap the other Transformers and make his escape.

Storm force
The wind speed inside a hurricane can reach a massive 200 mph (320 km/h). The winds can rip houses off the ground and do an enormous amount of damage.

Hot Shot and Wheeljack transform into vehicles to look for the treacherous Thrust.

The Mini-Cons' Secret

"Are you sure this is a good idea?" said Alexis anxiously, as if she had already made up her mind what the answer was.

Rad, Carlos, and Alexis had left the Autobots' ship and were now on the surface of the planet with their three Mini-Con friends, High Wire, Sureshock, and Grindor.

Friends united
Human friends Rad, Carlos, and Alexis met at their school near the Cosmo Scope Research Center—a huge telescope in the desert.

Rad

Alexis

Carlos

Optimus had ordered a retreat of all Autobot forces, and the place was crawling with Decepticons, making their expedition very dangerous.

The only good news was that the Decepticons were all busy searching for the traitor, Thrust.

"We have to get into those tunnels," explained Rad. "You saw what happened when Hot Shot reported in. Our Mini-Cons thought that they recognized those underground tunnels where he was standing. Maybe we'll find some answers to the Unicron mystery down there."

"I still think we should have told Optimus," said Alexis.

"He would only have said it was too risky," chipped in Carlos.

"Yeah," said Alexis, "He would probably have been right!"

Tunnels
The longest railroad tunnel in the world is the Seikan Tunnel, which runs between Honshu and Hokkaido in Japan. It is 33½ miles (54 km) long.

The kids secretly travel down to the planet in the hope of finding some answers.

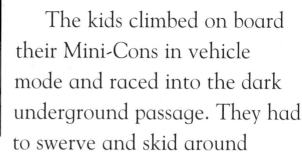

The kids climbed on board their Mini-Cons in vehicle mode and raced into the dark underground passage. They had to swerve and skid around places where the roof had caved in.

"This place is weird. It almost looks like it's organic," said Carlos.

The Mini-Cons were racing forward like they were in a trance, homing in on something.

It wasn't long before the group turned a corner to see the giant figures of Starscream and Thrust. Starscream had finally tracked down the traitor.

When Thrust saw the kids, he laughed and aimed the Requiem Blaster at them. In a desperate attempt to save them, Starscream leaped forward just as Thrust fired!

Partners
Each kid has their own Mini-Con. Alexis' Sureshock is a scooter, Carlos' Grindor is a skateboard, while Rad's High Wire is a BMX bike.

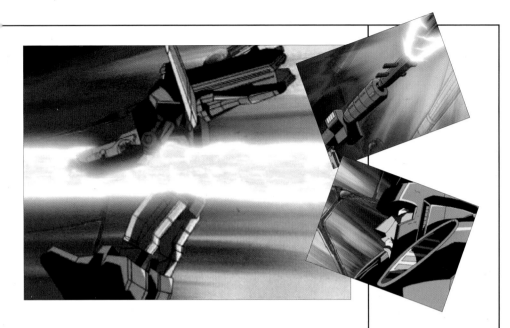

Suddenly, a blinding white light enveloped everything, and the kids screamed. It felt like something strange was happening.

The next thing that Rad remembered was waking up in the cavern again. But this time things felt different. All around them, trapped in the walls of the chamber itself, were the lifeless bodies of all their Autobot friends! What was going on? Why were they trapped?

Thrust fires the Requiem Blaster straight at Starscream, who only survives thanks to the strange power of the Mini-Cons.

Rad is astonished to wake up and see a strange vision of the Transformers.

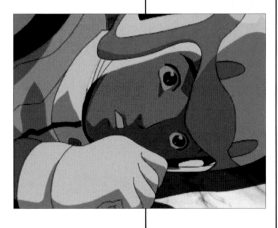

Inside the weird chamber, the kids look on in horror at the trapped bodies of the Transformers.

Creator
The origin of the Transformers race has always been shrouded in mystery. Could it be possible that the evil Unicron actually created them for his own devious ends?

The grotesque cave even included Galvatron and his Decepticons. It looked as if the walls had somehow been feeding off them.

Worst of all was the horrifying sight of Hot Shot, lying in the corner, half-consumed but still conscious. He didn't recognize the kids at all.

"Whoever you are, you'd better get out of here, before you get trapped like the rest of us," he cried.

"He doesn't know us," said Rad. Then he had an idea. "Somehow we've gone back in the past to millions of years ago, before we met the Transformers," he exclaimed. "How did this happen?"

"We were told that we could use the Mini-Cons, but it turned out that *we* were the ones being used. Who would have thought that the

Mini-Cons had been created by Unicron and were his servants!" explained Hot Shot.

"But why?" said Rad.

"Unicron feeds on hate and violence, and the Mini-Cons were designed to heat up the Decepticon-Autobot war! To make us fight to get them!"

The kids gasped.

Time travel
The kids are shown a vision of Cybertron millions of years ago, when Unicron had been in control.

Hot Shot explains to the kids that the Mini-Cons were created by Unicron.

Escape
Fed up with being caught in the middle of the Autobot-Decepticon war, the Mini-Cons fled Cybertron millions of years ago. All the Mini-Cons left their home planet on a special spacecraft.

There was another flash of blinding light, and the kids were moved back through time once more by the Mini-Cons' power.

The roof of the chamber was now covered in bright green globules, and the kids witnessed the amazing birth of the Mini-Cons— each one a cell from Unicron!

"But they can't be a part of Unicron! He's evil, and they're our friends!" cried Carlos, as the newly birthed Mini-Cons marched past the three kids.

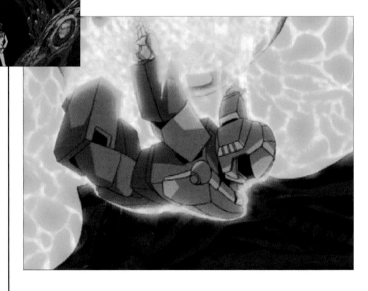

The kids see the Mini-Cons being born out of the cells of Unicron.

The Mini-Cons' spacecraft traveled far across the Universe using the Transformers' warp gates.

After millions of years on Earth, the Mini-Cons were woken up by Rad.

The kids were consumed by another flash of blinding white light and found themselves back in the present.

As Thrust and Starscream struggled for control of the Requiem Blaster, the gun unleashed a shot that brought the roof of the chamber crashing down.

While Starscream protected the humans from falling debris, Thrust made a quick escape.

"We need to get back to the ship," said Rad, grimly. "We have to tell Optimus Prime the news."

Crash landing
The Mini-Cons' ship crash landed on Earth, scattering the Mini-Cons all over the planet and the Moon.

The Moon
The Moon takes about 27 days to orbit once around the Earth. It is too small to have an atmosphere, so there is no wind or rain there.

Thrust warps out to Cybertron's moon.

After his escape, Thrust used a warp tunnel to meet up with Sideways deep inside Cybertron's only moon.

Thrust followed Sideways to the central chamber, where Sideways took the two weapons that Thrust had stolen from Galvatron.

"These will wake up our master!" said Sideways, pushing the Skyboom Shield and then the Requiem Blaster into place.

The effect was immediate! The central core began beating like a giant heart. The ground trembled and then shook with increasing violence. Something ancient and evil was stirring.

In the moon's core, Thrust wakes up Unicron with the Mini-Con weapons.

Down on the surface of Cybertron, all Transformers, Autobot and Decepticon alike, stopped whatever they were doing and stared up at the planet's moon in horror.

The crust of the moon was cracking and, slowly but surely, two gigantic horns pushed themselves up through the moon's surface!

It was then that the entire Transformer race realized the terrible truth… the bleak, cratered moon that orbited their world was, in fact, artificial. The moon itself was Unicron!

Jupiter's moons
The giant planet Jupiter has 60 moons. Its largest, Ganymede, is the biggest moon in the Solar System.

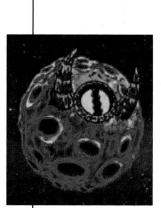

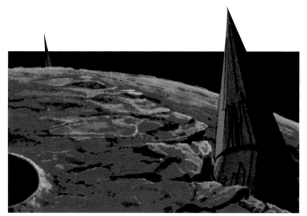

Cybertron's moon was transforming—Unicron was waking up.

Galvatron nearly defeats his Autobot archenemy.

Star Saber
This weapon is a powerful sword formed when the three Mini-Cons Jetstorm, Sonar, and Runway combine.

Below the sinister, horned moon, Optimus Prime was facing off with Galvatron on the battlefield. Optimus knew that this was his last chance to persuade Galvatron to join forces.

"How long have we been adversaries?" said Galvatron, taking a swipe at Optimus with the Star Saber. "It seems like since the beginning of time."

The two giants fought a ferocious battle, until, thanks to the Star Saber, Galvatron won the upper hand.

Just as it looked as if Optimus Prime was doomed, an explosion shook the battlefield.

"Starscream!" gasped Galvatron as the Transformer saved Optimus.

Starscream believed that the Decepticons and Autobots should unite to fight Unicron, and he was prepared to put his life on the line to prove it.

Galvatron and Starscream began trading blows, the blue Star Saber clashing noisily with Starscream's own sword Wing Blade. Neither of the two Decepticon warriors would back down until, in the heat of battle, Galvatron struck his former friend a deadly blow.

Wing Blade
Wing Blade is the powerful and unique sword wielded by Starscream. With the Decepticon's strength and skill behind it, it is even a match for the Star Saber.

Starscream and Galvatron battle fiercely with the Wing Blade and Star Saber.

Galvatron had thrust the Star Saber deep into Starscream's chest, and he fell to the ground, dreadfully wounded.

"Galvatron, you must listen. Do as Optimus says and join forces with the Autobots, otherwise every last one of us is doomed. Please sir, do it for me," rasped Starscream in desperation.

Starscream aimed his laser cannons upward and fired at the Unicron moon. The response from Unicron was swift and deadly— Starscream was enveloped in a destructor beam and was so badly wounded he became deactivated.

Starscream lies wounded, hit a terrible blow in the chest by Galvatron.

Brave Starscream's attempt to save the Transformers from Unicron ends in his deactivation.

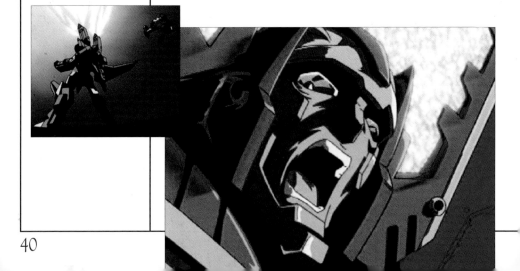

His friend's cruel fate shocked Galvatron more than he could say. He silently held out the Star Saber in the direction of Optimus. They would join forces to defeat Unicron!

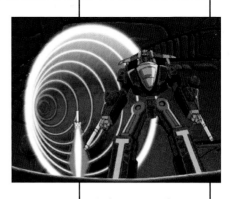

Sideways steals the Star Saber for Unicron and warps out to join his evil master.

Just as Optimus reached out to take the sword, a figure leaped from the shadows and grabbed it!

"Sideways!" exclaimed Optimus.

"This sword belongs to Unicron," shouted Sideways, warping out with the weapon.

It was a disaster. Starscream was deactivated, and now Unicron had all the Mini-Con weapons! How could the Transformers stop him?

Two faced Sneaky Sideways has often changed sides in the Autobot-Decepticon war. Was he trying to help out or was he making things worse for his own reasons?

Cyclonus
This trigger-happy Decepticon is always ready for a fight. He transforms into a high-powered army helicopter and can attack from the sky.

With the Star Saber now in place at its core, Unicron's increasing power caused a huge gravitational storm to hit Cybertron. The Autobots and Decepticons had to evacuate in a hurry, launching all their battle ships into space.

The two Transformer flagships docked, and Optimus and his men walked onto the Decepticons' vessel. The soldiers of both forces watched the scene as Optimus Prime and Galvatron exchanged a historic handshake. Now the Transformers were fighting as one!

"All ships…to Unicron!"

The assembled space fleet headed straight for the evil Unicron and fired a barrage of light bullets and lasers.

Every ship fired its weapons, and each Transformer blasted away with his individual armory.

When the smoke cleared, though, the fleet was astonished to see that Unicron was completely undamaged.

"Whoa! We didn't even scratch it!" gasped Jetfire.

"If we're going to have a chance against Unicron," said Optimus Prime. "We need to rethink our strategy and find his weak spot."

For the first time in their history, the Decepticons and Autobots join forces to defeat a common enemy. Optimus Prime and Galvatron shake hands on the deal.

Jetfire
This Autobot sometimes acts as Optimus's second-in-command and can transform into space shuttle mode. He can combine with Optimus to form Jet Convoy.

The Transformers take Discovery Pods and land on Unicron.

Demolishor
Demolishor is Galvatron's most loyal follower, obeying Galvatron's orders without hesitation. He can transform into a missile tank.

Optimus Prime ordered Hot Shot, Side Swipe, Demolishor, and Cyclonus to take a Discovery Pod and land on Unicron. The team's mission was to explore the surface of the transformed moon and find a possible weakness.

Optimus had guessed that the tiny ship would slip safely through Unicron's defense systems unnoticed. He was right. When they landed, the team split up and headed in different directions.

As they explored, suddenly the whole moon shook, and huge cracks appeared in its surface.

"Unicron is changing again! He's coming to life!" said Optimus on the bridge of the fleet's flagship.

"We must open fire on him! This may be our only chance!" said Galvatron urgently.

"What about the landing team? They'll be killed!" said Rad.

Galvatron was ready to accept them as casualties of war, but Optimus had other ideas.

"We'll despatch a rescue mission!" he ordered. "Let's hope it gets there in time!"

The moon's surface started to crack as Unicron begins his final transformation into giant robot mode.

Side Swipe
Side Swipe is an emotional Autobot, who was taken under Hot Shot's wing. His Mini-Con partner is Nightbeat.

The landing team is surrounded by Unicron's droids.

Defense droids
These flying, ball-shaped defense droids travel in swarms. In enough numbers, they can be a deadly match for any Transformer.

Optimus in jet mode launches an aerial attack on the droids.

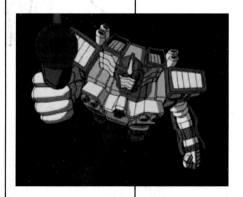

Unicron had begun fighting back against the intruders on his surface, and Hot Shot, Demolishor, and the team soon had to retreat.

"Power link! Jet Optimus transform!" shouted Optimus and blasted off into space, heading for Unicron.

On the surface of Unicron, Hot Shot and the landing team were now surrounded by Unicron's defense droids. Just as the droids were about to open fire, Optimus Prime swooped out of the darkness and blasted the droids to pieces. Flying behind Optimus, to give him cover, was Galvatron! The two leaders grabbed their men and flew them to safety.

Unicron continued changing into his true, terrifying form.

What remained of the moon's surface was jettisoned into space. Huge mechanical limbs began to emerge from within.

The gigantic form of Unicron was now revealed for the first time. He was the size of a planet! His fiery red eyes stared out from a face of pure evil, promising death and destruction to all who opposed him!

To be continued…

Unicron
Unicron is finally revealed as a huge mechanical being. Will the united Transformers be able to resist his evil plans?

The true form of Unicron is revealed for the first time.

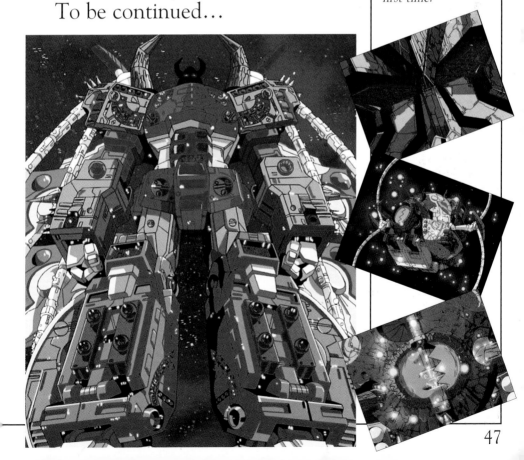

Glossary

Atmosphere
The layer of gases that surrounds a planet. Earth has a breathable atmosphere.

Black hole
A collapsed star from which not even light can escape.

Conscious
Being awake.

Cosmos
The entire Universe.

Deactivate
To stop a machine from working.

Devastation
Complete ruin.

Digital
A form of information that is coded into digits, or numbers.

Escalate
To make something bigger or more serious.

Expedition
A journey undertaken by a group for a special purpose.

Ferocious
Extremely fierce or savage.

Flourishing
Doing very well.

Foe
An enemy.

Galaxy
A group of billions of stars.

Globules
Round lumps of a sticky, semiliquid substance.

Gravitational
Forces to do with gravity. Gravity is the force that makes things fall to the ground.

Grotesque
Horribly ugly.

Hibernation
Time spent (usually in winter) in a sleeplike state.

Military
Anything to do with the waging of war and the army, navy, marines, or air force.

Milky Way
Our own galaxy, containing the Sun and billions of other stars.

Moon
A natural body that orbits around another larger body, such as the Moon around Earth.

Organic
Relating to living matter.

Origin
The beginning.

Pawn
A person used by others for their own gain.

Polar
Relating to the poles of a planet. Earth has two poles, the North Pole and the South Pole.

Stalemate
A situation that neither side can win.

Static
An electric charge that is usually created by rubbing two things together.

Strategy
A plan for a battle or other activity.

Telescope
An instrument with a lens that is designed to make distant objects look nearer.

Trade
Exchange.

Trance
A semiconscious state.

Unique
One of a kind.

Unleash
Let go.

Veteran
A person who has had experience in a particular field, such as war.

Wield
To hold and to use a weapon or tool.